THE VALUE OF ADVENTURE

The Story of
Sacagawea

BY ANN DONEGAN JOHNSON

The Value of Adventure is part of the ValueTales series.

The Value of Adventure text copyright © 1980 by Ann Donegan
Johnson. Illustrations copyright © 1980 by Value
Communications, Inc.

First Edition
Manufactured in the United States of America
For information write to: ValueTales, P.O. Box 1012
La Jolla, CA 92038

Library of Congress Cataloging in Publication Data

Johnson, Ann Donegan.
  The value of adventure—Sacagawea.

  (ValueTales)
  SUMMARY: A brief biography emphasizing the value of
adventure in the life of the Shoshoni Indian woman who
acted as a guide for the Lewis and Clark expedition.
    1. Sacagawea, 1786-1884—Juvenile literature.
2. Lewis and Clark Expedition—Juvenile literature.
3. Shoshoni Indians—Biography—Juvenile literature.
4. Adventure and adventurers—Juvenile literature.
[1. Sacagawea, 1786-1884. 2. Shoshoni Indians—
Biography. 3. Indians of North America—
Biography. 4. Adventure and adventurers]   I. Title.
F592.7.S123J63   970.004'97 [B] [92]   80-17623
ISBN 0-916392-59-7

1 2 3 4 5 6 7 8 9 84 83 82 81 80

THE VALUE OF ADVENTURE

The Story of Sacagawea

VALUE COMMUNICATIONS, INC.
PUBLISHERS
LA JOLLA, CALIFORNIA

This tale is about the adventurous Sacagawea. The story that follows is based on events in her life. More historical facts about Sacagawea can be found on page 63.

Once upon a time...

in the long ago years when much of our country was still a wilderness, a little Indian girl named Grass Woman was growing up in the rugged territory where Idaho and Montana meet.

Grass Woman was a Shoshone Indian. Her people were hunters and horse traders. In the summer months they lived in the high country, eating berries and fish. In the winter, when the snow blanketed the mountain meadows, they drove their horses down to graze in the warmer valleys, and they hunted wild game there.

They had to move their camps often so that the herds would always have fresh grass, so the Shoshones did not plant crops. They did not build houses. It was a wandering, uncertain way of life, but it suited little Grass Woman very well.

"I never know at the beginning of a day how that day will end," said Grass Woman. "Perhaps that's what makes life so much fun—not knowing exactly what will happen."

"Sometimes it would be more comfortable if we did know," said her mother. "Right now I would like to be sure that we will have some berries to eat for dinner."

"We will have berries," declared Grass Woman. "That is, we will have berries if I can find any." And she ran off to look for berries in the bushes that grew close to a swift-running stream.

Did she find berries? She did not. But she found something much better. She found salmon. The plump, sleek fish were battling their way up the river. They leaped clear of the water, and then fell back again with great splashes.

"Oh, great!" cried Grass Woman. "Salmon are much better than berries! At least for today we'll have plenty to eat!"

With that she plunged into the water to catch a fish.

Grass Woman laughed with glee when she threw a fine big salmon out of the stream onto the bank. "I like the way this day is turning out," she said happily.

"Wouldn't it be nice if all adventures ended as well?" said a small voice near the edge of the water.

Grass Woman blinked. At first she could see nothing except a round green stone on the river bank. Then the stone moved, and Grass Woman saw that it was really a little green turtle who sat there staring at her with its bright yellow eyes.

"Of course, adventures don't always turn out well because adventures are rather risky," said the turtle. "That's what an adventure is, after all—a thing you do even when you can't be sure what the result will be. I myself am very fond of adventures. I'd never get anyplace if I stayed safe inside my shell, would I? I have to stir about and put my neck out and take risks."

"I don't believe this!" cried Grass Woman. "Turtles don't talk!"

"Are you sure?" laughed the turtle.

"I'm sure," said Grass Woman. "I think you're a make-believe creature. I think I'm imagining you. But even if you aren't real, you're a funny turtle, and maybe you're wise. I'll take you home with me and we'll see what we will see."

11

Grass Woman carried the turtle home. She named him Walking Stone, which seemed to be an excellent thing to call a turtle.

From that day on, the turtle was always with Grass Woman. He went along when she searched for roots that might be good to eat. She took him berry picking and fishing. Whenever the Indians broke camp and moved to new grazing lands, the turtle moved too. He traveled on top of Grass Woman's bedroll.

As the summer drew to an end, the Shoshones began a long
trek to the East, to the place known today as the Three Forks of the
Missouri River.

"When we reach the river," said Grass Woman, "the men will ride
out across the plains to hunt the buffalo."

"That will *really* be an adventure!" cried the turtle. "I've never
seen a buffalo. I'm looking forward to it!"

When the Shoshones made their camp near the river, Grass Woman and Walking Stone watched the men get ready to go hunting.

"Isn't this exciting?" said Walking Stone. "Do you suppose one of the braves might want to take a willing and adventurous turtle along?"

Grass Woman was about to say that she really didn't think so. Before she could speak, however, she heard the pounding of hooves on the plain. There was the thundering roar of rifles, and several Shoshone braves fell to the ground.

"Run, Grass Woman!" shouted her father. "Hide yourself! It is our enemy, the Minataree Indians! Run! Run for your life!"

Grass Woman ran. She heard the guns again, but she did not look back. She splashed into a stream and struggled to reach the tall reeds on the opposite side. "If I can hide there," she said, "they may not find me!"

But then she heard hoofbeats close behind her, and a mighty splashing as a horse galloped into the stream.

"Oh no!" cried Grass Woman. "Oh, help me! Help!"

15

There was no one to help.

A Minataree brave leaned from his horse and seized Grass Woman. He swung her up in front of him.

"Let me go!" screamed Grass Woman.

The Minataree only laughed. He wheeled his horse around and raced away from the Shoshone camp, and he carried Grass Woman with him.

Grass Woman was jolted, bruised and out of breath when she reached the Minataree camp with the Indian who had captured her. She was so frightened that she could hardly keep from crying. But she felt a little less alone when she saw that some of her friends were also prisoners of the Minataree. There was the little girl named Leaping-Fish Woman, and there was Otter Woman, too. Four Shoshone boys had been taken prisoner in the raid. One of them was the tall, strong boy named Elk Horn.

The Shoshone children huddled together that night while the Minatarees celebrated their victory over the Shoshones.

"I'm afraid my father was killed," said Grass Woman sadly. "I don't know what happened to the rest of my family."

"I don't know what happened to mine, either," said Leaping-Fish Woman.

Poor little Otter Woman said nothing at all, but her eyes filled with tears and she began to cry.

"Don't cry," said Elk Horn. He leaned close to Otter Woman. "It isn't hopeless," he whispered. "We can watch for a chance to get away, and then we can run back to our own people."

Otter Woman dried her eyes when she heard this. Grass Woman felt a little comforted, but she knew it would not be easy to escape.

"The Minatarees will be watching day and night," said Grass Woman to herself. "What if we try to run off and we are caught?"

"It will be an adventure," said a familiar little voice near Grass Woman's foot. "You can't be sure it will turn out well, but isn't freedom worth a risk?"

"Walking Stone!" cried Grass Woman. "I'm so glad to see you!"

"It took me a while to catch up with you," said the turtle. "I have some good qualities, but speed isn't among them."

"You are fast enough—for a turtle," said Grass Woman, and she sounded almost happy.

There was no chance to get away that night, and the next day the Minatarees broke camp and began to journey toward the east. There was nothing the Shoshone children could do but follow, and so they did—all that day and the next and the next. They were many miles from the Shoshone camp where they had been captured and Grass Woman began to fear that she would never see her own people again.

As time passed, however, the Minatarees did not watch the kidnapped children so closely. At last Elk Horn came to Grass Woman.

"Tonight we must try to escape," said Elk Horn. "We will push those logs into the river, and then we will hold onto them as they float downstream. In the darkness, the Minatarees will not notice that we are gone—not until we are far away."

"It will be dangerous," said Grass Woman, "but we must try."

That night the Shoshone children stretched out in the shadows and closed their eyes. They waited. It seemed a very long time before the Minatarees were asleep. The moon was high and the night was very dark when the Indian camp was quiet at last.

"You may have some problems," Walking Stone whispered to Grass Woman. "It's true that your captors are asleep, but so are most of your friends."

"Never mind," said Grass Woman. "I'll wake them."

And she did, very quietly. "Don't make a sound," she warned as the Shoshone children went, one after another, to the safety of the river.

At last only Otter Woman and Leaping-Fish Woman remained sleeping in the Minataree camp.

"Careful!" warned Walking Stone, as Grass Woman crept close to Otter Woman. "If you startle her, she might call out."

"Otter Woman, wake up!" whispered Grass Woman. "It's time to go!"

Otter Woman opened her eyes. "What?" she cried. "Who's that? What's the matter?"

The Minatarees heard her. Instantly the Indian camp was in an uproar. Braves raced off into the night to look for the Shoshone children who had gotten away. Squaws crowded around so that Grass Woman and her friends could not move.

"So much for the great escape," said Walking Stone. "This adventure didn't turn out well at all."

"Perhaps we can try again, later on," said Grass Woman.

25

Later, when Grass Woman and her friends were living in the Minataree village, there was another chance to get away.

"Let us go now," said Leaping-Fish Woman. "The Minataree no longer watch us so closely. They will not miss us until we are far from here."

Grass Woman knew this was true, but she shook her head. "You go," she told Leaping-Fish Woman. "You are quick and nimble, and your legs are strong. You can run so that the Minataree will not overtake you. But Otter Woman's legs are bent and she cannot run. If we both leave her, she will be alone here. I will stay with her."

Leaping-Fish Woman hugged Grass Woman. She cried when she said goodbye, but she went. Grass Woman sat down beside Otter Woman and took her hand.

"You are a brave girl," said Walking Stone. "You could have escaped with Leaping-Fish Woman."

"It will be a different sort of adventure to stay with the Minataree, won't it?" said Grass Woman. "We don't know how it will turn out, do we? We shall wait and see."

The Minatarees were farmers as well as hunters and trappers. As time passed, they taught Grass Woman and Otter Woman to plant corn, to tend it, to harvest it and to bake bread.

"You work hard, Grass Woman," said Walking Stone one day. "When you aren't tending the corn, you are making deerskin moccasins or scraping buffalo hides. What do you think now of your adventure with the Minatarees?"

"I think it was more fun to roam free, the way I did with my Shoshone people," said Grass Woman. "But I am used to hard work, and the Minataree brave who captured me is kind enough. We shall see. Perhaps something exciting will happen before long."

No sooner had Grass Woman spoken than there was a stirring and a bustling among the Indians. "The white men have come," said one of the women. "They will trade for our furs. Come and see, Grass Woman. They bring guns and bullets and beads and blankets."

Grass Woman had never seen a white man before. She hurried to watch a French trader named Toussaint Charbonneau. He was using sign language to speak with the Minatarees.

29

"That white man has been here before," said one of the Minatarees. "He loves to gamble. Just watch him!"

Grass Woman and Otter Woman did watch. They saw the Frenchman playing an Indian game with the brave who was their master. As he played, Charbonneau looked up from time to time and smiled at the Shoshone girls.

"There's something about this that I don't like," said Walking Stone, and the turtle crept to hide under a hollow log.

Just then Grass Woman's master made a loud noise. It was a disappointed, unhappy sort of noise. The Indian got up and came toward Grass Woman and Otter Woman.

"I have done a very foolish thing," said the Indian. "I have gambled with the Frenchman and lost—and so I am not your master any longer. He is! He has won both of you!"

Grass Woman stared at Charbonneau, and Otter Woman began to tremble. "What will happen to us?" Otter Woman whispered.

"Who knows?" said Grass Woman. "Be brave, Otter Woman. Perhaps it will not be so bad. Perhaps it will even be exciting—it will be another adventure!"

The next day, Grass Woman and Otter Woman left the Minataree village with Charbonneau. They journeyed eastward for many days until they came to a village where some Mandan Indians lived. Charbonneau made this place his home when he was not trading with the tribes to the west.

"I am afraid," said Otter Woman to Grass Woman. "What will these strange people do to us?"

"I do not think they will do anything bad," said Grass Woman. "Why should they? And our new master will protect us, for surely he wants us to work for him."

Of course Grass Woman was right. The girls were soon busy curing buffalo hides for Charbonneau. They sewed clothes for him and made his deerskin moccasins. They cooked his food, planted his corn and dug roots which the Frenchman might use for medicine.

"I think I like it here," said Otter Woman one day. "Even if we have to work hard, there is always plenty to eat."

"There may be plenty to eat here on the plains," said Grass Woman, "but life with these Mandans is even more dull than it was with the Minatarees. These people never move around! They live always in one place!"

Grass Woman tried not to be discouraged. She was a bright, quick person, and she managed to keep herself fairly cheerful. Soon the Mandans decided that Grass Woman was not the right sort of name for her.

"She must have a new name," said the Mandans. "We will call her Sacagawea. That means Bird Woman. The name fits her, for she moves like a sparrow or a wren. She is never still."

"That's a nice enough name," said the girl. "But does it really matter what I am called? One day is like another in this village, and nothing exciting happens. Changing my name will not really help."

"Wait and see," said Walking Stone. "I have a feeling that you will have adventures in your life—wonderful adventures!"

Sacagawea was about sixteen at this time. She had been living among the Mandans for five years. It was so long that it seemed the Shoshone camps of her childhood were like distant dreams. The dreams became even more distant when Charbonneau decided that he would take Sacagawea and Otter Woman as his wives.

"Is this an adventure?" said Sacagawea to Walking Stone. "If it is, I do not like it. Charbonneau is too old to be my husband."

"It is not the sort of adventure I had in mind," said the turtle.

While Walking Stone and Sacagawea waited and hoped for something to happen, there was great news in the far-off city of Washington.

The year was 1803, and the French Emperor Napoleon Bonaparte had just sold the vast area called the Louisiana Territory to the United States. The new lands reached from the Mississippi to the Rockies, and from the Gulf of Mexico north to Canada.

"We now possess thousands of square miles of wilderness," said President Jefferson. "What we must do is explore the area, and perhaps also find an overland route to the Pacific."

The President chose two brave soldiers, Captain Meriwether Lewis and Captain William Clark, to lead an expedition west across the continent.

"You will be doing your country a service," the President told the men, "and no doubt you will have an unforgettable adventure."

"Let us take great care that the adventure will succeed," said the men. Then they began to enlist other men—men who were brave and skilled, and who were adventurous enough to want to be among the first to cross the American continent.

In the spring of 1804, Lewis and Clark set out from St. Louis. At that time, many people believed that it might be possible to reach the Pacific by following the rivers of America, so the explorers started north on the Missouri.

There were thirty-two soldiers and ten civilians in the expedition. Lewis and Clark had mountains of supplies and the best equipment money could buy. They had a keelboat which was fifty-five feet long, and they had two pirogues. These were like huge canoes, and they were propelled by sails and oars.

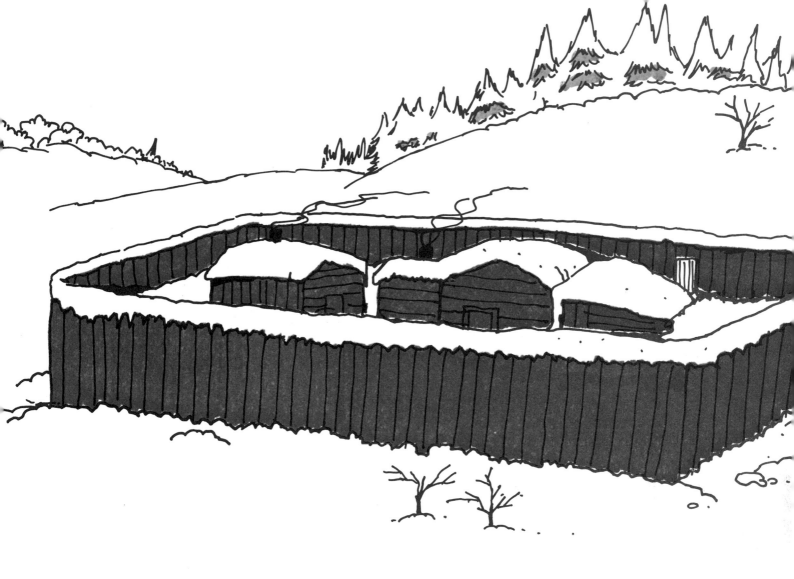

"Every man who can should keep a diary," ordered Captain Lewis. "If we reach the Pacific, our journey may become a part of history. It's important that we write down everything that happens."

They voyaged on through the wilderness for 1,600 miles. Then, as winter closed in upon the plains, they reached the place which is known today as Fort Mandan. It is near the site of the present-day city of Bismarck, North Dakota.

"We cannot go further until spring," said Lewis. "The wind is bitter, and soon the river will be frozen over."

So the explorers hauled their boats out of the water, and they built shelters for themselves on a stretch of land near the Mandan village where Sacagawea lived. They put up a stockade around their huts and waited for spring to come again.

While they waited, snug in their fort, the adventurers talked of the hardships that might be ahead and of the preparations they must now make.

"You will need an interpreter," said the Frenchman named Toussaint Charbonneau. He had come to the fort to see what the white men were doing. "There are many Indians between here and the Pacific. I can speak to the Minatarees for you. And my wife Sacagawea is a Shoshone. The Shoshones live beyond the mountains and they have many horses. You may need horses before you are through."

Lewis and Clark soon realized that Charbonneau was a braggart who did not really understand the Minataree tongue. They saw that the Frenchman needed Sacagawea beside him if he was to interpret for them.

"But can we take the Indian woman with us?" said Lewis. "She is about to have a baby. Do we want an infant on the expedition?"

"Perhaps we have no choice," said Clark. "If we are going to communicate with the tribes to the west, we'll need her. And if we take her, that no-good husband of hers must come, too."

And so it was settled. Charbonneau was to be the interpreter and he was to bring Sacagawea on the journey.

Sacagawea was busy then, helping the men to get ready for the trip. She made new moccasins and she mended leather tunics. She put aside great piles of dried corn and beans, and she smoked the meat of deer and buffalo. And while winter still held the land in its grip, her baby was born.

"A son for me!" said Charbonneau, who was terribly proud of the little boy. "I will name him Jean Baptiste. That is fitting for a French child."

"And I will call him Pomp," Sacagawea whispered to Walking Stone. "The name means 'leader' in Shoshone, and I know that he will be a leader. How can he help but be a leader? He will be part of this wonderful adventure with Captain Lewis and Captain Clark."

"Yes, it will be a wonderful adventure," said the turtle. "I knew all along that something really great would happen to you. Do you plan to take me along on this trip? Or must I stay at home by myself?"

"You know that I will take you," said Sacagawea. "When I talk to you, you understand, because you are really my own thoughts. How could I go anywhere without you?"

At last the spring came to the land. The ice on the river broke up and warm winds melted the snows. It was time for the expedition to move west.

Otter Woman came to the edge of the river to say farewell to Sacagawea. She sighed as Sacagawea put the baby Pomp on her back. Pomp was snug and warm inside his Indian cradle.

"How I wish my legs were straight and strong, so that I could go with you," said Otter Woman.

"I will miss you, Otter Woman," said Sacagawea. She embraced her friend, and then she took her seat in the white pirogue. "Do not forget me while we are apart," she said.

Captain Lewis gave the order to start, and the men in the pirogue dipped their oars into the water. The pirogue began to move.

"I am so excited," whispered Sacagawea. "I can hear my own heart beating. It's a little frightening though, isn't it?"

"All adventures are a little frightening," said Walking Stone, who sat beside Sacagawea and watched the river flow by. "It has to be frightening when you really don't know what will happen. But think of it! Before another springtime, you may see the broad Pacific!"

"I may see my own people again, too," said Sacagawea.

This thought was always in her mind as they traveled westward through the wilderness. The days became weeks, and spring turned to summer. Sometimes the rain pelted down and Sacagawea had to shelter her baby as best she could. Sometimes the sun was burning hot and she had to cover Pomp with her blanket.

"What a good little boy you are," she whispered in the Shoshone language. "You never complain."

Of course, Pomp didn't answer. Sacagawea was glad that her make-believe friend, Walking Stone, was along. If it hadn't been for the turtle, she would have had no one to talk with.

One day, when Charbonneau was at the tiller of the white pirogue, a strong wind blew suddenly out of the north. It caught at the sail of the boat and tilted the pirogue over to one side. Water poured into the boat, and the supplies which were stowed in the pirogue began to tumble out and float away.

46

"Help!" cried Charbonneau. "I can't swim!" He jumped up as if he would leap into the river.

"Watch out!" cried Captain Lewis, who was walking on the riverbank. "You'll turn her over. We'll lose our supplies!"

But then Lewis saw that Sacagawea was snatching packages and boxes out of the water as they began to float away.

After a moment, Charbonneau managed to control himself. He and the other men got the pirogue back on an even keel so that no more water poured in. They bailed the boat dry and stored the supplies properly again.

"You were the only one who kept calm when the pirogue upset," said Lewis to Sacagawea. "You have more courage than any of the men. If it hadn't been for you, we'd have lost everything."

Sacagawea felt very happy. "The captain spoke to me as if I were someone important," she whispered to Walking Stone. "At last, I'm really part of the adventure."

"You've always been part of the adventure," said Walking Stone. "The captain just didn't realize it until now."

The explorers pushed on until they came to the foot of a great waterfall. There they stopped and Captain Lewis looked at the torrents of water that thundered down over the rocks. "We've already left the keelboat behind," he said. "Now I think we must leave the pirogues. As for the canoes, we'll have to carry them up past the falls."

Some of the men set to work then, hauling the pirogues out of the river and covering them with brush. Others joined Captain Clark, who was going ahead to explore the land beyond the falls.

And while the men were so busy, what was Sacagawea doing?

She was sitting as quietly as she could, holding little Pomp and clutching a blanket around herself.

"What's the matter?" said Walking Stone. "You've told me a hundred times about the great falls near the land of the Shoshones. You are almost home, Sacagawea. Aren't you excited?"

"Yes, I am excited," said Sacagawea, "but I don't think that that's the reason I have such a pain in my stomach. I'm afraid that I'm really sick! Oh, Walking Stone, what will happen to my baby if I die here on this journey?"

50

Walking Stone could not answer. He could only wait and watch while Sacagawea grew sicker. Soon her fever was very high, and none of the medicines which the white men had brought in the pirogues did her any good. For ten days the Indian girl lay in great pain. She could hardly sleep, and she could not eat a thing.

At last, Captain Clark returned from his explorations. "The Indians at Fort Mandan spoke of a spring of sulphur water near the great falls," he said. "Perhaps that would help Sacagawea. At least it can't hurt her!"

Clark found the spring and he brought the water to Sacagawea and coaxed her to drink it. It seemed to help. Soon she could sit up again.

51

Then she was well enough to walk about the camp with her baby on her back. She watched the men bustling about, getting ready to move the canoes and supplies up past eighteen miles of falls and rapids to the river above.

First the men cut down several big trees. They sliced round pieces of wood from the tree trunks. Then they used the masts from the pirogues for axles, and they put together a pair of makeshift wagons. At last they loaded the canoes onto these wagons and hauled them up the slope past the falls.

It took weeks for the explorers to get all of their belongings to the high country. By the time they finished, Sacagawea was as strong as ever. And when she reached the top of the falls with her baby, she was so excited that she trembled.

"You see that place there?" she said to Walking Stone. "That is where the Minataree rode down on our camp. And there! That is where I was captured. And those hills over there—those are the mountains where my people lived in the summer. I hunted berries there, and I dug for roots and . . . and . . ."

Sacagawea stopped, for she could not speak any more.

"There now," said Walking Stone. "Perhaps soon you will see the Shoshones again. Perhaps some of your family are still alive."

Lewis and Clark were also wondering when they would see the Shoshones. "Your people are horse traders," said Lewis to Sacagawea. "Soon we will need horses. I see now that we can't travel much further by canoe. If we are to get across the mountains, we must ride—or walk."

Sacagawea pointed ahead. "There is another river beyond those hills," she said. "In the summer, my people live beside that river."

Lewis nodded. "I'll take three men and go ahead by foot," he said to Clark. You can follow with the canoes."

Lewis and his little band of explorers trudged ahead through the wilderness. After three days they saw a party of Indians. They made signs to tell the Indians that they came in peace. They also tried to say that they needed horses, and that soon canoes would come with the beads and blankets that would pay for the horses.

The chief of the Shoshones was named Cameahwait, and he seemed to understand the white men. "At least he isn't hostile," said Lewis to his men. "But we need Sacagawea. She can really talk to the Shoshones for us."

Days passed as Lewis waited with the Shoshones. Sometimes the Indians were friendly. Sometimes they were suspicious. At last, Clark and his men appeared on the river near the Indian camp. Of course, Sacagawea was with Clark.

Lewis stood surrounded by Shoshones, and he saw Sacagawea hurry toward him. Her face was bright with joy and there was a lightness to her step that had not been there before.

"Leaping-Fish Woman!" she cried. "It is you. You are safe!"

"Grass Woman!" called an Indian girl who hurried to meet Sacagawea. "I am so happy. When I had to leave you with the Minataree, my heart felt as if it would break!"

Now the Indians were suspicious no longer. They knew that Lewis and Clark could not be enemies, for they had brought Grass Woman back to her own people. As Leaping-Fish Woman and Grass Woman embraced, the white captains were led to the tent of Cameahwait.

"But we must have Sacagawea with us," said Lewis. "We cannot talk without her."

56

At that, one of the men went to fetch Sacagawea. She came quietly into the tent of the chief, and her eyes were cast down, as was becoming for a modest Indian woman.

But then she looked up. She saw Cameahwait and what do you suppose she did?

"My brother!" cried Sacagawea. "Cameahwait, my brother!" She ran to the chief with tears of joy on her face. "I have come back to you, my brother!" she said.

"Astounding!" said Lewis. "Our interpreter—and she is the sister of the chief."

After that, there were no more questions. The white men would get the horses they needed. Cameahwait even promised that he and his people would help Lewis and Clark carry their equipment across the mountains.

But then Sacagawea learned that her brother and his people planned to leave Lewis and Clark to ride to the plains to hunt buffalo.

"They must hunt, for they have no food," said Sacagawea to Walking Stone. "But if they leave the captains, the white men may perish here in the high country. And surely, if the Shoshones abandon them, the white men will never come among my people again. What will I do? Can I help the captains without betraying my people?"

"Perhaps not," said Walking Stone. "Perhaps you must make a choice between them."

So Sacagawea did make a choice. She chose to warn Lewis and Clark that the Indians might desert them.

"How can you do this to us?" said Lewis to Cameahwait. "You promised to help us get our baggage to a camp across the mountains. Now are you going to abandon us?"

"My people are hungry," said Cameahwait. "If we do not hunt buffalo, we may starve. But what you say is true and I am a man of honor. I will keep my promise. We will not leave you until you are safely on the other side of the mountain."

Cameahwait went to call his braves together and he turned his face away from Sacagawea as he went.

"He knows that it is I who betrayed him," said Sacagawea sadly. "He will never look at me again. I am an outcast among my own people. But I did only what I had to do."

"Don't be unhappy," said Walking Stone. He spoke in as comforting a way as he could manage. "Once Lewis and Clark have found the way to the Pacific, white men will come again and they will trade with the Shoshones. Perhaps then the Shoshones will become a prosperous people like the Mandans."

Sacagawea knew this was true, and she felt somewhat happier as she and Pomp joined the explorers on their trek westward.

Before her journey was over, Sacagawea was to stand on the shores of the Pacific and look out across the ocean. She was to know that the white captains who had become her friends had succeeded. They had found a route across the continent. And, because she loved adventure and was willing to take risks and endure great hardships, she had been able to help.

When you think of Sacagawea, you may wonder about yourself and your life. Do you go ahead and try things, even when you aren't quite sure what the results will be? Are adventures important? Of course, no one wants to be reckless, and it's silly to take foolish chances, but can a sense of adventure help you to do worthwhile things? And can't it make life more interesting—and lots more fun?

The End

SACAGAWEA
1786–

Sacagawea was a Shoshone, born about 1786 in territory which is now part of the state of Idaho. When she was about eleven, she was captured by an enemy tribe. Some say that she was then sold to the Missouri River Mandans, who in turn sold her to a French Canadian fur trader named Toussaint Charbonneau. According to other accounts, Sacagawea's Indian captor lost her to Charbonneau in a gambling game. The facts are obscure, but there is a tradition that Sacagawea had a chance to escape at the beginning of her captivity, but that she chose not to leave her friend, Otter Woman.

Charbonneau, who lived with the Indians at the Mandan villages on the Missouri, took both Sacagawea and Otter Woman as his wives. Both girls were at the villages when Captains Meriwether Lewis and William Clark appeared on the river in 1804. The white men were heading a large party of explorers, and were on the first leg of their journey to the Pacific.

Always eager for money, Charbonneau applied for the position of interpreter to the expedition. He was accepted, and it was agreed that Sacagawea would accompany him on the journey.

The explorers left the area of the Mandan villages in April 1805. Sacagawea had her baby, Pomp, on her back. The child had been born in February, and his birth had been duly recorded in Captain Lewis's journal.

Four months after they left Fort Mandan, the travelers reached the high country beyond the Great Falls of the Missouri. Lewis explored in advance of the rest of the party, and he met the Shoshones who had been Sacagawea's people. The Indians were suspicious until Clark came into view. Sacagawea was walking ahead of the other explorers, and Clark wrote in his journal that she "showed every mark of extravagant joy" at the sight of the Shoshones who surrounded Lewis.

"A woman made her way through the crowd toward Sacagawea," Clark wrote, "and recognizing each other, they embraced with the most tender affection."

The woman had been Sacagawea's childhood companion. She had been taken prisoner with Sacagawea, but had later escaped.

Sacagawea found not only her old playmate in the Shoshone camp, but also her brother. He was Cameahwait, the Shoshone chief, and when he saw Sacagawea with the white captains, he promised the explorers horses and guides so that they could cross the mountains and complete their journey to the sea.

Before Lewis and Clark could take advantage of this promise, Cameahwait changed his mind. He decided to take his braves and go hunting, thus stranding the white travelers.

When Sacagawea told Lewis and Clark that Cameahwait might abandon them, she severed all ties that bound her to her own people. She allied herself completely with the white men. No doubt she very much wanted the expedition to succeed.

Cameahwait was persuaded to postpone the hunt, and to help the Americans, who then could go on across the Rockies to the Clearwater River, a tributary of the Columbia. Two months later, Lewis and Clark reached the ocean.

We know almost nothing of Sacagawea's life after the expedition. In 1812, a wife of Charbonneau died at Fort Manuel in the Dakota Territory, but this may have been Otter Woman. Tradition has it that Sacagawea lived to be very old, and that she traveled widely in the West. We cannot be sure. But we do know that if it were not for this remarkable Indian girl, with her courage and her love of adventure, the great journey of Lewis and Clark might never have been completed.

Other Titles in the ValueTale Series